My Own Big Bang

Jean Yamasaki Toyama

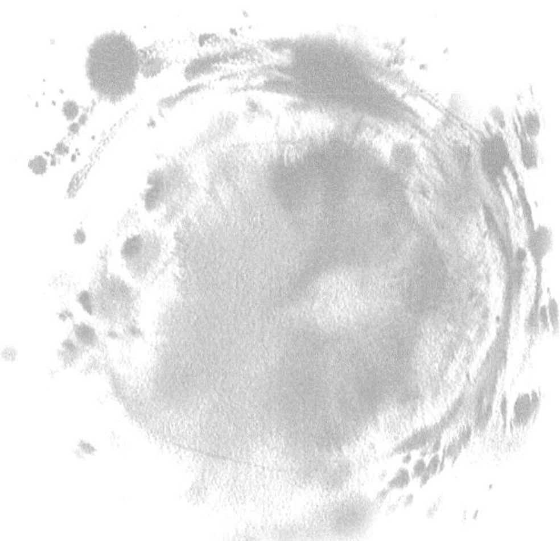

CYBERWIT.NET
FOUNDED 2000

My Own Big Bang

ISBN: 978-93-6354-645-5

Book designed by Jui-Lien Sanderson

Published by Cyberwit.net.

Printed at Repro India Limited.

CyberWit.net
HIG 45 Kaushambi Kunj, Kalindipuram
Allahabad - 211011 (U.P.) India
http://www.cyberwit.net
Tel: +(91)9415091004 +(91) (532)2552257
E-mail: info@cyberwit.net

In Memory of my mother, Fumie,
and my father, Tsutomu Yamasaki,
who caused my own big bang

TABLE OF CONTENTS

Body Lessons

How much easier to lie there and watch than to be watched and to act. How much easier to lie and lie and become one with the lying, to be a part of the bed.

Just a little nudge, you gave me a nudge,
a nudge you gave me, nudge me,
nudge
to urge some forward movement
toward where I am to go
go on to where I had not gone
nor was going, dilly dallying
on to where I was not going

You nudged a little because I tarried
long, along the way where no way
just a circling around in circles
just a nudge toward forward
where I was to go

Just a little nick, a nick in
time, a nick of flesh, a nick
not long, but big enough
to take it out that bit
that tiny, incy wincy bit
of cancer.

Me who can assign meaning to shit falling on my head from a passing bird can't help but believe my cancer a meaningful event. The most obvious would be that proverbial wake up call, but then my uterine cancer did not perceptibly change my life, no doubt because the culprit was removed in totality and could not threaten. Now, the breast remains—or the remains of the breast can still threaten, can once again, at any time, move into action, to invade the rest of my body. So, this is what they mean by life-changing event? My life didn't change the first time; will it now?

First my grandfather died of cancer; then his son, my father; then my grandmother, his mother; then their son, my uncle. My last remaining uncle, my father's brother, also has cancer. He and I are still living.

I receive a card written in my own hand and wonder if it is just another rejection form from a publisher. Already I feel disappointed—my name written in my own hand—certainly another rejection. It is the card from the Women's Center, the one I filled out when I went.

No checks on the other possibilities just on one:

__Negative/stable
__Your mammogram varies

__Additional imaging studies
_x_ Due to an irregularity on your mammogram, a more thorough evaluation is necessary. Please contact your personal physician or other health care provider as soon as possible to schedule the appropriate follow-up tests.

> Hurry, hurry, call your doctor
> It's growing, growing inside you
> beside you, in spite of you
> Call, call, hurry, hurry

I learn more about breast cancer than I ever cared to know, especially about the odds:

> See the risk sheet:
> post-menopausal
> 50% increased chance,
> without pregnancies add 50 more
> and, oh, japanese, another 3%
> like wine?
> you're lucky, take 35-50%
> estrogen?
> Bingo! for 10 years, that's all.
>
> if a walker, 25% chance of shit falling on your head

if a soprano, 30% chance of turning bald
and, oh, 50% chance of
can
can
can, oh can
that's good I can,
cancer

They took out 28 grams of tissue in all, 11 from the initial biopsy and 17 from the reexcision, in other words, the second cut. How much cheese is that?

My tiny, tiny—1 mm or .1 cm of invasive carcinoma—bit of cancer, microscopic almost, almost not but still there, highly aggressive, unresponsive to estrogen. The pathology report reads like this:

"Breast-invasive carcinoma information
Operative procedure: Right breast lumpectomy.
Tumor-histologic type: Invasive ductal carcinoma.
Histologic grade (S-B-R grade I-III): Grade III"

In my own way I have been an arrogant person, arrogant because timid, not wanting to do things to bring attention to my self, shunning advice to keep out of sight, believing I could avoid mistakes. The only time I listened was when I wanted to learn how to do something. I remember my gut reaction to my calligraphy teacher. I knew nothing about Japanese calligraphy but when he took my hand to show me how to do the simplest and the hardest character— one, *ichi*— a straight line, I had to force myself not to react. How stupid! Who was wrong, my body or my mind? Now I want to learn to survive, not to die from cancer. Who will teach me, my body or my mind?

Perhaps it was the early death of my father that has made me so acutely aware of our eventual end. I cried myself to sleep for almost a year. It hurt so much that he would not share my graduation from high school, my triumphs in college, my marriage, my success, my children. I doubt I thought of that. He who used to carry me on his back when I suffered with toothaches, who drove us to school, who worried about our future as he lay dying for all those months.

He must have regretted all those events that he would miss more than I could ever imagine as he lay there in bed feeling his very strength leak out of every pore. A slow death is a blessing for the family. It prepares them for the departure of the beloved. In the end one thinks, At last! But for the departing it must be slow torture. To lie in bed, look out the window, count the daily passage of the sun thinking all the while, I am dying, I will be dead soon, what have I done with my life? To fill those last months with regret.

Only forty-five, he was only forty-five. When I passed that age, I prepared for death. I expected it. Cancer of the stomach. Cancer of the throat. Cancer of the head. I had symptoms galore in expectation of my demise. Every year for five years, beyond the age of forty-five, I thought this is it. This is my time. It never happened. I was relieved, but as I approach another decade, Kenko, that Japanese philosopher, reminds me. "We cannot live forever in this world; why should we wait for ugliness to overtake us? The longer man lives, the more shame he endures. To die, at the latest, before one reaches forty, is the least unattractive." I am not Japanese. I cannot think this way.

Imagining death and oblivion, a better alternative to disappointment, regret—whatever—doesn't play in some confined compartment of the brain. I flirted with death like the romantics I studied, confident of the years yawning before me. Now I want to marry life. No playing the field. No longer just going steady. I want a real commitment to being.

So much information, so many choices. To cut the nodes or not? To radiate or not? To take Tamoxifin or Arimidex or not?

Learn to do what is necessary to switch off the cancer-on button. Doctors don't know why some cancers turn on. The potential to kill is always there. Turned on, they do, turned off, they don't. I want to stop this on off switch. Oh yes, some days, I slip into that I'd rather be dead mode, but I don't mean it. I've got to be in better communication with my body, so it doesn't say no when I really mean yes.

It's not the C-word
that crawls under our skin
that keeps our eyes wide open at night
it's the R-word: recurrence,
repetition, repeat, reappear, remain. . .
you cur.

The trouble with cancer is that it's never over when it's over, unless of course that over is: "You're dead." Even if you miss the first death sentence, you are imprisoned for life.

Sorry, sorry, sorry for myself, I am, and feeling quite justified to become one with the bed. To become sloth—oh, yes, sloth—let my fatigue reign. Why? I have a good excuse—cancer—how convenient. I am my disease. I can become this terror, this fiction, this real end—sorry.

I'm already buried in a box. Lying there before the moving coffin—it's eaten me alive. Once the screen flickers, I am engulfed by other lives and their stories, poundage lost, lovers gained, careers made and all the products I should buy and adventures I should seek, elsewhere. I've always missed the place I'm not, never loved the place I am. Teach me, teach me, cancer dear, the place where I am at.

Part I
THE UNIVERSE

Before the Big Bang

There was no then then
no before before
but maybe only now
which is not even now
but past
then there was no past
no future
no now
no time
because nothing had yet begun
there was no beginning.

So when does begin
become begun?
Only after the Big Bang.

When?

Is there a now at the edge of
the universe, when it all started with
the big bang? We won't know
because the light from the now
took billions of billions of years
to get to our eyes. By now, that now
is not now. What we see is a then.

What Is the Universe Made Of?

Protons and neutrons were thought to be
basic.
Then came the quarks:
two up, one down is a proton;
two down, one up is a neutron.
4 forces:
gravity,
electromagnetic,
strong force,
weak force.

If we only knew as much
about human matter.

Flash

Before I knew it
the now was already
gone.
It moves,
irretrievable.
Unknown before the knowing.
There is no now now
all is only past or future
live in the now
they say,
but it doesn't even
exist.
It's gone
before you say
the word.

Now

Physicists say that one day,
when we look up into the sky
there will be no stars,
at least we won't see them.
They will have been pulled outward
by the cosmological constant,
that's not so constant,
since it increases, even by
infinitesimal degrees,
thus each star moves away
from each other.
All stars and thus planets will be
isolated.

We'll be alone in the dark.
So enjoy the skies now, while we can.

Look

Far beyond the moons
of Jupiter
you can see the stars,
the galaxies,
the clusters of galaxies,
and if your eyes are really
good, you can see
inside yourself

Two Worlds

The universe invaded my head
full of galaxies of milky ways,
red giants and worm holes
hollowing out the spaces of my brain
The convolutions spread open for
asteroids, the menninges
spread open for moons and the rings
of Saturn take their turns
in spinning my mind
in circles
round
round
unbound.

It Makes me Hungry

for the big and the small of it
for the fast and slow of it
for the hot and cold of it
for the ins and outs

of the whys and wherefores

Words Make It So

Papahānoumokuākea,
the name just ripples off my lips.
What a treasure! A reminder of the sacred
ʻOumuamua, a messenger from afar
arriving first Kamoʻoalewa,
oscillating celestial object,
Kaʻepaokaʻāwela, mischievous,
opposite-moving companion of Jupiter
Pōwehi, black hole, embellished
fathomless dark creation
Hawaiian and the Kumulipo are forever
linked to the stars and the seas.
How appropriate!
Hawaiian navigators used the stars
to find their way on the seas.
May we be able to navigate
the universe with the TMT.

Unseen

In the whole scheme of things
things are mostly invisible
the extragalactic background light (EBL),
the cosmic microwave background (CMB),
dark matter, dark energy mostly theory . . .
mystery all around
In other words,
you are the only mystery
you can solve.

So solve!

Part II
THE WORLD AND ME

The Hōkūle‘a

"The ancient Hawaiians were astronomers."

Queen Lili‘uokalani

I see it, right before my eyes,
as waves break on both sides
of the twin hulls of the Hōkūle‘a
cutting through the waters:
Diamond Head.
It looms into the sky
towing a string of lights.

It would have been
a dark silhouette then, draped
with a crown of stars.

Now, too much light . . .
Stars barely visible in today's Waikiki skies.

How many stars could they have seen, those
Hawaiian voyagers,
when the skies were clean of
earthly light?
I imagine them at sea, like me now,

watching the sky kiss the waves.
My body trembles: I blink hard.
They were in the dark
with nothing but these mute
guides offering direction.
Look! I see the Little Dipper with
the North Star hanging on its tail.
I feel the spray of sea
as we cut through the water,
we'll soon return.
I think about the ancient ones
— nā po'e kahiko —
robust, curious, hungry to find.
How they would have relished
exploring the Milky Way
— Hōkūnohoaupuni—
to watch creation unfold
by slicing through time
diving into the waves of
the Big Bang.

Sight

Lemaître, you hadn't yet proposed
the "Primeval Atom"
but, well, looking at our stars
I somehow think that you knew that
we are all connected
and that our bones,
our sinews, and our blood
somehow remember
our starry source.
I'm looking at the stars
so bright in the morning night
advancing towards the dawn
so fast, so fast
into the light,
stars still there but
unseen by these
aging eyes. I saw them
better long ago
when there was not so much light . . .
when my eyes were stronger.

Scattering Light

Gone the howl of winds
The steady collapse of skies

Quiet on the firmament
she rises from the wound
making cunning music for the stars

A flood of blistering, roiling
light streams out in tongues
continues the work begun
from the deep of Pele's belly.

Heart Sick

"That is longing for the sea"
writes Langston Hughes.
It makes you toss around in bed
as if you were on the ocean
rocked by the movement of
the earth beneath the water.

In your heart
you are moved.

Song

It sings. What sings?
The morning sings
with sounds of coming alive
filling the space of dawn with flickers
of coming, alighting, resounding.
I am filling with awake! the blood
of hello, of get up to breathe.
No matter what . . .
the morning brings the sense of alive.

Wings

I write this poem on the fly,
the wings of a fly
buzzing in between
my convolutions
my everyday
resolution
that I will write
a poem a day

Music

A little bit of cheer
that's all we need to buck
up and hold fast. We don't
ask for much, just a few
notes of ups to cut out
the downs. With morning comes
the jazz of work, the symphony
of sirens and the hip hop of city noises.
A bit of word jujitsu can make things just
right.

Pleasure

I never knew the pleasure of quince.
The florist had to tell me. Now
each day I look at my branches (she said
I chose a good bunch). I see the pink
open wider here,
a tiny dot of green peeks out
from a crease there, buds turn pink.
Each day I watch something emerge.
Sprout!
The joy of quince:
you watch it bloom
not die.

What Artists Do

Just an old turnip
not smooth like the skin of a babe
nor gnarled to look like Christ
a plain old turnip
but Odilon Redon transformed
that simple vegetable
into something to contemplate
something beyond an old turnip

Kusama, My Hero

Nothing comes of nothing.
So Yayoi works everyday
to make something out of
nothing with polka dots that she
fills with more polka dots, a landscape
of something, a world full of rounds
and rounds on top of rounds
filling holes on a canvas
to make a space come alive.
to make something out of nothing.

Create, He Said

"I watch the ground of my mind
and a lotus will rise from the mud."

I watch and I watch,
see nothing but dust
ground up fine
good only for concrete
and thick.

My Gratitude

My gratitude sometimes slakens
I do not remember all that I should.
My gratitude sometimes flattens
without the muscle of deeds.
My gratitude has been fickle,
coming and going,
smiling and weeping:
a barometer of my mood.
I am grateful to my bones
but sometimes I don't feel it.
Today, I do.

He‘e

I imagine he‘e oozing out
of a half-inch hole sliding
in front of me, all 8 undulating
legs of him, he‘e slithering out
of sight into another hole
and then here comes honu,
nonchalant, turning his
head towards me flipping his
tail in good-by, slipping
between the coral,
his head sliding
into his shell.

Fickle Lover

Go away, Potote, you are too
close. The yellow fish keeps
circling me. I turn away and
think him gone, only to find him again
next to me like some unwanted lover.
I lift my head out of the water and
flag my sister: "There's this yellow
fish following me around!" and point
to the water. She looks
at me and continues.
Unafraid, he stays near, I assume the "he".
"He's still following me!"
She looks up and nods her head.
We continue all across Hanauma Bay.
He sticks with me.
Beyond the patch some waves roll over me
and he's gone. I look around: no where.
I see my sister rushing out of the water.
"What's the matter?" I shout.
She says, "There's this yellow fish
following me!"

Adoption

It came right up to my goggles, like it
had been waiting for me to plunge into
Hanauma Bay.
So close to the glass of my face mask,
I had to adjust my eyes.
I tried to shoo it away,
but within a minute it returned.
I swam among the coral for a few minutes,
sure it would go, but then
there it was right in front of my face.
Does it think I'm its mother?
Everywhere I turn it comes into my line
of sight. No other fish like this around:
just this golden yellow, black striped
fish with a stripe across the eye.
We swam the bay together.

Visitor

He appeared there on my mirror.
I didn't recognize him. Such a shock!
A wiggly lizard, baby lizard, there
on my mirror. No doubt frightened.
I gently lifted him and took him to the lanai.
Stunned, he lay there.

When I returned to the lanai,
he was gone.

Lying beneath my mirror,
a tiny tail.

I see him again.
He's found a home
in the center of a pineapple crown,
growing on my lanai
He must have believed he was nice and safe.

I bend down
just to say hello.

He jumps
and disappears.

Fish Spotting

There is a spot on Pier 7 right
by the Falls of Clyde
at the edge of Aloha Tower Marketplace.
There you can see exotic tropical fish
outside of a tank. Passersby might look,
but they don't stay.
Me, I throw bread into the water
and watch the yellow tang—lau'ipala—,
the moorish idol—kihikihi—, and those
brutish scrawled filefish—loulu—
vie for the crumbs. I've seen a few
barracuda and one shark, but I missed
the whale that wandered into the pier.
Too bad for me.
Never mind.
There's lots to see
at the pier.

Alike

The fly is a sly bugger.
Some are house flies,
others, dog dung flies.
They have one thing in common:
all are attracted to decaying material.
In other words,
flies like shit.

Imagine

Let's imagine,
our community black hole
receiving society's errors
erased from our collective
memory so that we can
heal. And our own personal black
hole welcoming the memory
of all our mistakes.
Sucked out of mind.
Hello, Peace.

Will to Fight

Where will it come from?
From the head?
the eyeball? the heart?
No, not the heart,
worn out the heart,
better the stomach
that's where
the guts are.

Recycle

Last June I came across
a carcass,
some misshapen ball
of once live fuzz
now unidentifiable:
a car had crushed it.

With a guava stick
I prod that odd heap
to turn the other side
towards the sun.
Inside like minature plumerias,
a world of shimmering white
consuming as it moves in dazzling union
the unknown flesh
transformed from death
to new creation.

This shape that once was otherwise
now houses
a different universe.

Inspired by Bashō's Travels

Travelling along this twisted road,
I look back
at all the signposts
followed or ignored and sweep
my eyes along the curves and curbs.
What made me stop
here at this path, lined
with weeds and an occasional can
with jagged cover.
Was it to pick up the rubbish?

Trek

It's been a long trek to where
I'm going, a destination not yet
in sight though I'm following
that road, the one I chose.
Not there yet, I tell myself, go on,
go on, don't stop.

Kaput

My computer went kaput!
Can't log on. Screen frozen.
Do desperation act: reset
system management
controller (SMC). Pray.
Nothing happens. Screen still
frozen. Call Apple. No solution.
Get appointment with Genius.
Pray. Go to Apple. 10 minutes.
"You were pressing the wrong
side of the mouse. Left
not right."

Just Right

Time eats us up,
with every small bite
we are less and less the whole,
less and less that person
we are trying to become.
In self-defense we should
perhaps be content with
being instead of *becoming*.
To be, truly and fully,
is enough.

On the Izu Peninsula

I pick up a slice of sashimi
from the body of this whole fish
expertly displayed with head in tact
belly sliced and exposed. A succulent
piece, poised on my chopsticks
ready for my mouth
I see the tail flip back and forth.
Its mouth and eyes wide open
it glares at me as if to say,
That's my body you're eating.

Travel

I'm looking at the Eiffel Tower. I'm upside
down
in a head-pose on the lawn of the Champs de
Mars.
Drunk. Raoul and I finished the whole bottle
of pinot.
"Your eyes are the color of wine," he says,
"so *crépusculaire* in the twilight."
The smell of fading chestnut blossoms
hangs in the air.

He hands over the joint and smiles,
"Hold it in as long as you can."
Wisps of smoke escape his lips.
I don't know his name.
Where are we I wonder?
Is that thundering water I hear?
I remember Gocta Waterfall.
Oh, yes, we're in Peru.

I read that travel dims your wit . . .

suddenly I'm an old woman.

What the Heck!

It sings. What sings?
The morning sings
with sounds of coming alive
filling the space of dawn with flickers
of coming, alighting, resounding.
I am filling with awake!, the blood
of hello, of get up to breathe.
No matter what . . .
the morning brings the sense of alive.

Magic

My magic carpet of words
will take me from this busy
place to some other quiet
one where there is peace
from the comings and goings
of the world, where I can be still
and still be happy.

Awake

I woke up this morning,
be thankful,
the roof was still attached,
be thankful,
my legs moved,
I walked,
my mouth talked,
I said I love you.
I got out of bed!
be thankful,
I am alive
and I wrote a poem.

Be thankful!

Part III

ME AND ME

My Own Big Bang

Embedded in an unnamed file,
moved to trash
left there years ago,
found on a memory stick,
left in a box, discovered on an old mac-mini
lying unplugged on a desk in the corner
retrieved from a 4½ inch
plastic card-like thing
whose name I can t remember
originated on a floppy disk
inserted in a Kaypro,
illuminated by the cosmic microwave
background radiation of my own big bang
I recover the flash of old poetic creations.

Look

Far beyond the moons
of Jupiter
you can see the stars,
the galaxies,
the clusters of galaxies,
and if your eyes are really
good, you can see
inside yourself

Make

What is it that wants to emerge,
to find form, to be released,
to be born?
What is it that needs being,
to be seen, to be heard,
to be felt?
What is it that has been hitting hard,
hitting soft,
sleeping in
sleeping out?
What is it that has been quiet,
that has spoken loud,
You.

All Right

When things don't go right but
swerve severe right,
I need to shake off the disbelief,
clear out the denial,
face the mourning,
and get stronger
and smarter
for the next round.

Gift

If only we were gifted with
that magic that brings back the past,
better than it was,
maybe then
we could remember

How Do I Mind My Mind?

I am not in my perfect mind
these days. You know why
as much as I. How then
to transform that imperfection
to something less mangled
by these times?
How to mind my mind?

I must mind
more up than down
more sweet than sour
more good than bad.
That's how to find
my perfect mind.

Gift

How about a poem today
a short one
a sweet one
one that comes from
your heart
all green in its glow
of virtue
or indigo from
the middle eye
or purple from the
top of your head

Do It!

If I had a poem somewhere, I'd pull it out
of my pocket
my purse
my happiness....
Share with my friends.

He said it right,
Bradbury did,
you are a writer, if you write
and find joy in putting one word
next to the other,
blackening the page
with words
like a kid with paint.
Get dirty.
That's all.

Inspired by Iijima Koichi

I'd like to write a poem on a long bandage and
soak it
in ice water to cool down.
Things are getting too hot even where
flowers are blooming on old
magnolia trees and oysters still survive
in too warm waters. I'm not a fascist
so this heat is not pleasant.
I don't want to destroy my country.
Just want to be able to
write my poems in peace.

Vocabulary

I learned the word, wizened,
in the 11th grade and liked
how it blew out of my lips
and brought images
of witches
and winds out from
my depths
now it's me,
a wizened me

Cold Mountain

Now I stand on a cliff looking out toward
a stretch of mountains.
All hangs there in the sky of my mind, while
the roots of an old Cyprus tree grow
between my toes
and the branches embrace me
like a sister.
Weeds have started to penetrate my skull
I feel them burrowing through my hair
insinuating themselves between
the fissures of my skull.
Soon they ll be growing inside, then
curling out of my eye sockets

On Reading Han Shan

If I had gone to that cold mountain
and found my way without a path
and if I had stayed the way I wanted to
I would have become a part of the craggy rocks
grown into the crevices
embraced by the roots of the cypress tree.
And I would be able to see the stars
at night, maybe those galaxies too.

There would be no light
from cities
no houses on the mountain
just me, the rocks.
and the old cypress tree

Advice

You tell me to boil simple foods
for my body
to read ancients texts for my bones
here in my concrete mountain
in a modern city
long years grow short
warm bones grow cold
but if I can still laugh and sing,
I'm not
that old.

My Gratitude List

i have food to eat.
a roof over my head,
a car with some gas,
my utilities are paid,
i have social security
and retirement, my
100 year-old-mother
wants to live 4 more years,
she's happy, i can still
sing in tune most of the time.
But these last few weeks
are sucking up the marrow
of my poetry. There won't
be much left for osso buco.

Look!

There is a poem here, somewhere
in the words,
hidden in a syllable,
capped in a vowel.
Look under that consonant.
It s there.
The sound of it, caught
in your ear like a buzz, stuck in your pipe,
like a fish bone, there in the soft
flesh of your throat.
That word, it s there.
Cough it out!

Sewing

If not but by a thread
how would it all hold?
If not but by a thread
how would the path
be made clear?
If not but by a thread
how would I be able to stitch
this story through
loop by loop
word by word
and tie it
all together.

Fly

I blinked and already two days have passed
two days without a poem
it goes so fast
the days
the chances to write
a poem
so catch it before it flies away.

I write this poem on the fly,
the wings of a fly
buzzing in between
my convolutions
my everyday
resolution
that I will write
a poem a day

Books, Books, Books

I lose my books in my library
in those sort-of-arranged shelves
not alphabetical
no categories
just books I like
books I should like
books I've forgotten I had

Shelf

It will collapse again, the new one, I mean.
Too loaded, too many.
It's listing, listing.
When will it fall?
When will this book
shelf give up
on me.

In the Cracks

I lost it somewhere in the crack
between the stove and the fridge
or maybe behind the
armoire where I can't
dust
(the ants have made a nest)
it might have slipped
under the bed or in between
the pipes behind the
sink
it waits
I know
till I can once
again regain it
take hold of
my missing
mind.

Just Right

Time eats us up,
with every small bite
we are less and less the whole,
less and less that person
we are trying to become.

In self-defense we should
perhaps be content with
being
instead of becoming.
To be truly and fully,
is enough.

Surprise

So this is how it happens:
a little grey at the temples, later
a white frame around the face,
then a slight sag under the eyes,
then the jowls.
The lines get deeper as the years
move swiftly.
Then one day you look
in the mirror and
your grandmother is
staring back at you.

Look!

It goes fast, you know.
Before you know it, it's gone.
That's what he said.
I smiled at my uncle as if I understood.
It's taken fifty years to understand.
So enjoy life, even now, Jean. The sun rises.
The wind blows. The mountains stand erect.
And sometimes it rains.
Everything is good, if you
make it so.

Just

Just a little nudge, you gave me a nudge,
a nudge you gave me,
to urge some forward movement
toward where I am to go
go on to where I have not gone
just dilly dallying.
You nudged a little because I tarried
just a circling around in circles
just a nudge toward forward
where I needed to go
And because you nudged
I went

Write!

If there is a poem here,
I'll pull it out of the air
put it on a wave
or scatter it in particles.
I'd pull a poem out of anywhere
your ear
your heart, even
your belly button,
if I could.

Inspired by Beckett's Worstward Ho!

Onward, on, then off again,
beyond the day of gone
when all is done and gone again
to start once more, for on
is never done.

For Wayne Booth and his Art of Growing Old

There is no art in growing old.
It is a craft honed by practice.
Stitch after stitch,
turn upon turn,
breath into breath.
The weaver, the potter, the glass blower
work to make. The practice is the life.
The life becomes art.

So I'm reading Chuang Tzu, Thomas Merton's Translation

Loved the words:
"Easy is right."

Right on, I say,
this philosopher can't
be wrong. So I'm right.
I'm taking it easy.

"Continue easy and you are right."

Hallelujah!

Chuang Tzu continues:
"The right way to go easy
Is to forget the right way
And forget that the going
is easy."

Oh, oh!!!

Relief

Isn't it great when you find
something you thought
you lost? Your heart
twisted thinking you were not
careful with that precious thing
now gone somewhere in the mess
of your books, your notes,
your papers all disorganized
and stuffed willy-nilly, not
alphabetized, not categorized
but looking neat. And it is that
neatness that is maddening
because it masks the real mess.
But I found it,
Happy days!

Make Something

Everyone needs to make something
whether beautiful or ugly.
We want to create something
unlike anything someone else has done.
No, that's not exactly true.
Some like to pick up pieces of paper
or maybe—like me—pick up a word
or smear a word across a page, no,
the word is not smeared, it's there
clearly, just put here,
for you to see,
I put these words here.
And you read them.

Thank you.

Acknowledgements

I would like to thank the people who have encouraged me and helped make this wish a reality.

I thank Eleanor Wilner who helped me know I am a poet.

I thank Juliet Kono Lee and Julie Ushio for their encouragement and steadfast friendship and the members of the Bamboo Ridge Study Group for their attention to details.

I thank Jui-Lien Sanderson for her expertise and dedication to help make real my project.

I thank my Facebook Friends who have read many of these poems and whose responses gave and continue to give me encouragement.

I thank Bette Uyeda and Peggy Cha, my sisters, who helped put this book together.

I thank Dennis Toyama, who keeps me on track.

About the Author

A native of Hawai'i, Jean Yamasaki Toyama is a Beckett scholar and professor emerita of French at the University of Hawai'i at Manoa. She has published two books of poems, *Kelli's Hanauma Friends*, illustrated with paintings by local artist Russell Sunabe, and another, *Prepositions,* with paintings by Cora Yee. She has also published a book of stories and poems, *Wild Elephants.* Her short stories appear in *The Piano Tuner's Wife.* She was awarded the Cades Award for emerging artist in 2018 and is one of the *renshi* poets awarded the Ka Palapala Po'okela Excellence in Literature, honorable mention, for *What We Must Remember*, in 2019. Her work often appears in *Bamboo Ridge.*

www.ingramcontent.com/pod-product-compliance
Ingram Content Group UK Ltd.
Pitfield, Milton Keynes, MK11 3LW, UK
UKHW041315190726
13845UKWH00025B/282

9 789363 546455